Thumb Position Repertoi

Intermediate pieces for cello and piano

Spielstücke mittlerer Schwierigkeit für Cello und Klavier

Pièces niveau intermédiare pour violoncelle et piano

Pat Legg &
Alan Gout

© 1997 by Faber Music Ltd
First published in 1997 by Faber Music Ltd
3 Queen Square London WC1N 3AU
Music set by Jackie Leigh
Cover design by S & M Tucker
Printed in England by Caligraving Ltd

ISBN 0-571-51802-8

To buy Faber Music publications or to find out about the full range of titles available
please contact your local music retailer or Faber Music sales enquiries:

Faber Music Limited, Burnt Mill, Elizabeth Way, Harlow, CM20 2HX England
Tel: +44 (0)1279 82 89 82
Fax: +44 (0)1279 82 89 83
sales@fabermusic.com
fabermusic.com

FABER *ff* MUSIC

UNBEATEN TRACKS

8 contemporary pieces for Cello and Piano

Edited by Steven Isserlis

ISBN 0-571-51976-8

Unbeaten Tracks for cello brings the diverse world of contemporary music within the reach of the less-experienced player (around Grades 4 to 7). The eight pieces in the volume – all specially commissioned by world-famous cellist Steven Isserlis – are written in an array of musical styles by some of today's most talented composers.

Steven Isserlis: 'I am delighted with this collection of weird and wonderful pieces – a collection that I hope will come to be viewed as staple repertoire for cello students, as well as fascinating encores for professionals (I'm already performing several of them regularly). One of the qualities that I find most appealing in this volume is the variety of musical personalities that shine through each offering …'

Carl Davis	*Elegy*
Lowell Liebermann	*Album leaf, Op.66*
Olli Mustonen	*Frogs dancing on water lilies*
John Woolrich	*Cantilena*
Julian Jacobson	*Hip hip bourrée*
Mark-Anthony Turnage	*Vocalise*
David Matthews	*Tango flageoletto*
Steven Isserlis	*The haunted house*

FABER *ff* MUSIC

Contents / Table / Inhalt

1. Parting

Pat Legg

2. Thema from Piano Sonata K331

W.A. Mozart

3. Hornpipe

Anon.

4. Spanish ladies

Trad.

★ This accompaniment may also be played on the guitar.

Con ped.

5. Wiegenlied

F. Schubert

6. Hornpipe

Anon.

7. Sarabanda

G. Tartini

8. A distant land

R. Schumann

9. Ave verum corpus

W.A. Mozart

Thumb Position Repertoire
Intermediate pieces for cello and piano

Spielstücke mittlerer Schwierigkeit für Cello und Klavier

Pièces niveau intermédiare pour violoncelle et piano

Pat Legg &
Alan Gout

© 1997 by Faber Music Ltd
First published in 1997 by Faber Music Ltd
3 Queen Square London WC1N 3AU
Music set by Jackie Leigh
Cover design by S & M Tucker
Printed in England by Caligraving Ltd
All rights reserved

ISBN 0-571-51802-8

To buy Faber Music publications or to find out about the full range of titles available
please contact your local music retailer or Faber Music sales enquiries:

Faber Music Limited, Burnt Mill, Elizabeth Way, Harlow, CM20 2HX England
Tel: +44 (0)1279 82 89 82
Fax: +44 (0)1279 82 89 83
sales@fabermusic.com
fabermusic.com

Contents / Table / Inhalt

1. Parting

Pat Legg

© 1997 by Faber Music Ltd.

2. Thema from Piano Sonata K331

W.A. Mozart

© 1997 by Faber Music Ltd.

This music is copyright. Photocopying is illegal.

4

3. Hornpipe

Allegro ma non troppo

Anon.

4. Spanish ladies

Allegretto, lilting

Trad.

5. Wiegenlied

F. Schubert

6. Hornpipe

Anon.

6

7. Sarabanda

G. Tartini

© 1997 by Faber Music Ltd.

8. A distant land

R. Schumann

© 1997 by Faber Music Ltd.

9. Ave verum corpus

W.A. Mozart

© 1997 by Faber Music Ltd.

10. Lascia ch'io pianga
Aria from 'Rinaldo'

G.F. Handel

8

11. Planxty Irwin

Carolan

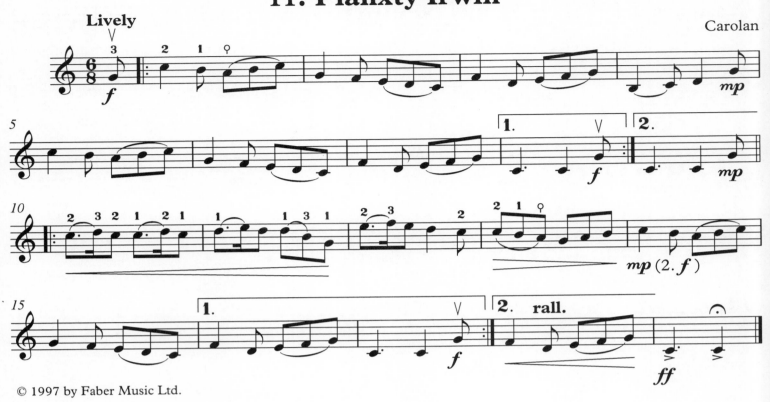

12. Adagio cantabile

G. Tartini

13. Tre giorni – air

G. Pergolesi

14. To a wild rose

E. MacDowell

[With a simple tenderness]

15. Moto perpetuo

Alan Gout

Vivo

16. Hornpipe

Trad.

10. Lascia ch'io pianga

Aria from 'Rinaldo'

G.F. Handel

11. Planxty Irwin

Carolan

12. Adagio cantabile

G. Tartini

13. Tre giorni – air

G. Pergolesi

Andante

14. To a wild rose

E. MacDowell

15. Moto perpetuo

Alan Gout

16. Hornpipe

Trad.

Steven Isserlis's
Cello World

HUBERT LÉONARD
The Donkey and the Driver

GABRIEL FAURÉ
Morceau de concours

SERGEI RACHMANINOV
Lied

ALEXANDER SCRIABIN
Romance

ANTONÍN DVOŘÁK
Romantic Piece

JULIUS ISSERLIS
Souvenir russe

ROBERT SCHUMANN
Intermezzo

SULKHAN TSINTSADZE
Chonguri

DAVID POPPER
Elfentanz

HEITOR VILLA-LOBOS
Song of the Black Swan

ISBN 0-571-51885-0

The cello as singer, as dancer, as folk instrument, even as donkey!

Cello World is a must for all cellists, a wonderful collection of original works and arrangements from the repertoire of world-famous cellist Steven Isserlis. The inspired line up of pieces includes Schumann's moving *Intermezzo*, Léonard's hysterical *The Donkey and the Driver* and Villa-Lobos' rippling *Song of the Black Swan*.

The music in this volume is recorded by Steven Isserlis with Thomas Adès (piano) on the BMG recording *Cello World* 09026 68928 2.

Also available from Faber Music:

Ludwig van Beethoven *Andante con Variazioni*   ISBN 0-571-51114-7
Ferruccio Busoni *Serenata, Op.34*   ISBN 0-571-51853-2
Ernest Chausson *Pièce, Op.39*   ISBN 0-571-51647-5
Camille Saint-Saëns *The Complete Shorter Works for Cello and Piano*   ISBN 0-571-51807-9
Carl Vine *Inner World*   ISBN 0-571-51748-X